SERIE d'ECRITURE

No. 30

Also by Paol Keineg:
Boudica, translated by Keith Waldrop, Burning Deck, 1994

Paol Keineg

TRISTE TRISTAN
AND OTHER POEMS

translated from the French
by Laura Marris and Rosmarie Waldrop

Anyart/Burning Deck, Providence

SERIE d'ECRITURE is an annual of current French writing in English translation. The first five issues were published by SPECTACULAR DISEASES in England. Since No. 6, the publisher has been Burning Deck in Providence, RI. Editor: Rosmarie Waldrop

Distributed by:
Small Press Distribution, 1341 Seventh St,. Berkeley CA 94710
1-800/869-7553; orders@spdbooks.org, www.spdbooks.org
www.burningdeck.com

Burning Deck Press is the Literature Program of ANYART: CONTEMPORARY ARTS CENTER, a tax-exempt (501c3), non-profit organization.

Cover collage by Keith Waldrop.

Parts of the translation of "Triste Tristan" have appeared in *Aldus, Asymptote, Broom Street Review, Ezra, Read: A Journal of Intertranslation,* and *Shearsman;* "Tohu," in *The Prose Poem;* "Among the Pigs," in *Golden Handcuffs;* "Abalamour: Because or Down with Love," in *The Brooklyn Rail inTranslation.*

3 1357 00243 0285

The poems were originally published as follows:
Triste Tristan, suivie de Diglossie, j'y serre mes glosses (Editions Apogée, 2003).
Tohu (Wigwam éditions, 1995)
"Among the Pigs," in *Là, et pas là* (Editions Le temps qu'il fait, 2005)
"The Berlin Wall" and "Abalamour" in *Abalamour* (Les Haut-Fonds, 2012), where they are attributed to Paol Keineg's heteronym Yves Dennielou.

Translation © 2017 by Rosmarie Waldrop and Laura Marris

SSN 0269-0179
ISBN 978-1-936194-24-7

CONTENTS

Triste Tristan (RW)   7

Tohu (RW)   47

Among the Pigs (RW)   53

The Berlin Wall or Blackberry Picking
in Western Brittany (LM)   57

Abalamour (LM)   77

TRISTE TRISTAN

They're still in our heads the good old fellows
let's talk hormones
a monologue of the deaf —
we allow a ration of free sex
down at the ford —
would have to be dumb not to sing
now
that the story's all over the world.

Béroul and Thomas,
of course we've read them,
bring up fornication
in every line —
a chance to embroider:
a tale of love won't always
lead
to sexual reproduction —
terror isn't the last word from heaven
we need the natives
for the lowdown.

Gains prestige
being on top of the queen —
she snaps, hurls insults
can't take it no more —
he, aggressive, comes —
two dogs stuck together
their talk
a slew of droppings —
I'll add a fool a dwarf a messenger —
as best I can.

Is nonetheless a cuckold,
par for a horse *—
jeers at the one he adored,
his face drenched with rain —
a spectacle with plenty of spies,
enemies of abstract art
forced to pipe down.

---

* Breton *marc'h* = horse

International debacle — this job of
the enraged husband —
beware the mangy cur, disgustingly
happy — good for nothing
howling at the merciful sky —
I get lost here, all these memories
and the piles of critical editions.

Stick it to me, your dick,
says Iseut (would you believe it) —
everybody believes it
to the point, precisely, where
God is hard pressed preaching love —
God, would you believe it,
rustling in flowing robes
and complicit —
otherwise how explain it —
they never stop,
he's going to kill her right there under him.

Iseut, black sky between her tits —
makes me hungry — me
who never thought I'd need
to throw myself on the bread —
this piece of Iseut:
thorax night,
tear at it with my teeth — likewise
smashed dishes
around them — something
makes them lose it.

Paneuropean Tristan
at the height of optimism
led by his horse —
first woman frenetic,
the second he can't fuck,
crisis:
down to the basement
closets at night —
don't linger here,
love, metaphysics,
that's what the police is for.

What we like is the hostility
of the barons hiding behind tree trunks,
the comm-
union with the woods, the sweat —
fear has its guardians,
Breton's a free tongue —
shall we go watch the kings
sail by in the bay?
lets take the shortcut.

Here where violence against animals
is not a legend
and readers start from the end,
where it hurts —
the stone in the forest
has come a long way —
we'll have to go far, very far
beyond the customary investigations
to find worse obscenities —
you mob of scholarly pedants
get the hell out.

Two steps
into the pornotopic forest —
Iseut on all fours initiated
into animal mysteries
by penetration —
can't say she doesn't work
at pure happiness —
the moment she
demeans herself
belongs to all of us as our own —
a background of revolt
worthwhile.

From the edge of the forest
they watch the harvest, the carting
dream of bread, eat it in dreams —
two lives that add up to a novel
where the lovers are loved by all
but the spies —
worse than a bitch
no way to pry them apart
their empty guts —
and God in all that?
he's not against it
provided he's loved too.

Squats down to piss in the micromoss
of xenoland:
if I'm beautiful
it's because my country's so shitty —
as I said: the habit of desire
has made a crime
of tentative gestures —
screams in writing
crime scenes without name —
the body, story of a screen.

So thin she no longer has breasts
craves a bit of soup —
we hear her noisy secretions
as far away as the islands —
if we could help her
could blow on the embers —
a skeleton thrown on the bed,
love demands you make love to her
on bended knee.

Tristan, Iseut, etc.
take nudity by storm —
the poor girl has escaped,
bursts of hate
all around the woods,
and the burghers
end up with a beautiful wedding,
the dog taken in with the loot —
the gift of oneself estranges the self,
we'd like to ruin
these militant lovers.

Joined
to the lady's ass
for hours —
poetry's can't-do-a-thing
no worry to him —
years near sovereignty
forbid his touching a corpse —
the forest experienced
as basis of
civilization —
the lady with the prominent nose turns into a scold.

Give weight to her breasts
lift them up with both hands —
life in the fields
a bit rough
with the pissing cows —
Iseut is sick to her stomach
of being torn open   `
belly to sell not for sale,
everyone's object of desire
lives under trees.

The moonlight again
so round, dispensing selves —
round, astonished eyes
see disant satellites —
funny how bloodless the real.

A cottage for two hearts —
mum or swearing,
they recoil from a unified tale —
the hermit in this remote place
is a foil of a good god good goddamn
good evening good teller of tales —
a pause in the Morrois forest,
can't stop pissing — he draws
his bow most tight, the arrow's for her.

Clavicle, sternum, breast of the man —
Iseut anal, oral, social, a sport,
pawed near the wells —
complains: get a move-on,
big savage — erogenous
zones planted with gorse —
read:
he marks his territory with piss,
she gets up on her hind legs.

Ear to the ground
strip bare whom you'll betray —
undress her ass
in the lyric tradition
screams sublimated
into scientific exhibits —
balls aching
for love of poetry.

Uniform pink
the tongue
deceives — glorious bodies
apart at the hip —
masterful brains
imagination
fueled
by the long fucks.

*Kelenn**, the teaching holly, doesn't teach —
she puts her head on his lap,
closes her eyes against sleep —
would be a great fragrant void,
an amphibian.

_____

* Breton *kelenn* = both holly and teaching

Set out in the morning to see the world —
quietly — love in time of war —
to put a posthumous world into French —
a God without a consistent method —
revolt against hierarchy
born of a bed of anger.

Joker of a dog dripping
salt water — across the sea, *tramor,*
a slave to sex
in a stinking land —
death, the world fucked up,
love globalized.

The blue of oyster beds,
the pink of penned-up pigs —
I don't travel without witness,
I know love by its pathology,
I've no science except nerves —
if you'd seen me hanging
on my mother's arm who was flayed alive
against a backdrop of comforting talk —
I was watching you from the corner of my eye,
sure of your ass, under the apple tree.

In this unfinished world
that we see with our soiled hearts —
their truant stammer
(we put those words in their mouths)
will always win out
over history's impotence —
signed: a man hardened
and gross, a fuckhead
thinking of thingumagigs
that reek of the foreign.

A fine mess:
Mark in a frothing rage
gets off his *marc'h*, his dead-tired horse,
straightens his aching back, his *kein*,
follows the *riboul*, the path to the *loc'h*,
made of *raden*, of *balan*, of fern and broom —
are we already in hell?
asks Mark,
I'm going to run my sword
through their mugs —
instead
tail between legs, he jumps
on his horse that slams on the brakes.

Hickies
on the beggar's neck —
it's really Tristan,
you've recognized
the young pack-o'-muscles
who's only after the crown —
endless loop of thighs —
spends his life spying on,
tracking,
straddling the queen's body.

Prefers Iseut to Iseut
and since the Iseut who's not Iseut
is called Iseut he marries her — she
keeps waiting in bed bare-assed
he, prisoner to a name,
can't get it up
for the Iseut who's not Iseut —
simply soft, his penis,
reduced to a proper name.

Time has passed; alright,
go on squatting at my door,
that's it, get used to it —
crawl back to your hole,
my hole's
not made for a child —
so what's this dog waiting for
at my door,
dying on his own turds.

Lack of religion is an article of faith
as he faces the crucial sea —
she won't come, he'll die, she'll die —
loc dislocated, locus that for now
has to take it.

To jump with both feet at the chance
for sin in the posthumous texts —
the void left by the end of love —
the end of the story makes her milk come in —
we prefer risking the body
to being riddled with revelation.

Happy with the war gear,
a few clouds, OK,
useless gray,
the two sides of bare skin —
eroticism is quietly slipped
into the lives of the poor.

Swifts
through the open window,
their carnivorous joy —
they swallow the light
by the hundreds every hour —
their screams stitch together
a white sky —
whereupon the forest trots out
the blue sky, the nightingale
with the golden hair in her beak —
let's strip down those spent lovers.

The meadow, big bed,
the power of the state authorities —
two deep footprints
in the sand —
big generic names:
chapel, beach, forest,
generate the history
of a streamlined myth —
love in the open air
at a gallop.

In the car that has served as your home
the dashboard's silent —
as you look straight at the island
you think of a pregnancy
in the 7th month stopped —
giving form to the rising water.

A small crowd of characters,
the moon in full daylight, pure
hearts crushed, there, where
we'll have to row across.

translated by Rosmarie Waldrop

TOHU

In memoriam Paul Quéré

From Keremma to Porz Meur. If I were I, I'd be happy to live in this crappy blue, far from all literature. Its lies foremost.

*

Happy sound, oh to lie down on it, on a mile of sea and light. White bands, rearview mirror. Smell of privet and manure. Alley-oop, with love, sandals, and hats gone with the wind. Let's run across the sand toward those blurry fishermen. How they lean into the wind, walking, and live the rhythm of tides.

*

At fifty, in one language, in another, and yet another, I'm doing well, I'm doing very well. I no longer adapt. Subdued, futile enough to kick at ruins. What do you say to the guys who head the pack? More light. And to those who bring up the rear and allow themselves to fall, fall again, and think divine thoughts?

*

Body within the law, bright birds in the sky of ideas. Down toward Kersioul, dog-roses, two lines by Kervarker written on the black-berries. The bay over there, sun thick as a callus, humming with work, heart of stone. What, no skipper in these waters? Nothing but parody?

*

Near Kervrezel, which no longer exists. I turned on my toes to see what's left. The flies are modernizing.

*

The winter over, it's winter still. The blackbirds envelop us in songs that end badly. I had my heart set on hearing a thrush. My mother said: the winter was hard, the thrushes are dead. Do I hear right? Come back, naive songs, country to drive one crazy. So much cruelty out of the towns, out of the mouths of people.

*

The well-trimmed trees touch the ground. I had written something else, but we've scorned them enough, the poor old folks, this winter sky in the midst of summer. Crack the whip, and the crowd, abused, will abuse. The sky all movement, black and grey, so quick the words come out by themselves. You think of what you have lost, you never get over it.

*

By the tree trunk, the flagpole. Past master in shackling. By the two ears. Hands bound by services rendered. They yield up work in sounds, on the dry side, slim. Are puzzled. Go howling past clouds dressed in red. Like warring wild boars. Like gusts that raise the dust

.   *

On ignoble roles. On the failure of capital entertainment. Slander of evil days. Have fought with, have left with. Now, and again, my name carries weight. My name of saddle, backbone, broad shoulders. The child I perhaps was did not see the night approach, nor the thieves. He left in good health.

*

Did you see, this morning, how the sun embraced the triumphal chariot of the slaughterhouse? Chicken coops, pig sties, always at the heart of our devotions. Soul turned to capital, with the last memories of childhood. Tomorrow is Caesar's. Today, with glassy eyes, we follow the wars in action.

*

On the god of battles, no comment. On his reek, his athletic rump in a sweat, no comment. On his deals, doublings, and provinces, no comment. On his well-dressed kids in the first row, no comment. On their pleasures, their laughs, no comment. On their games, their exquisite taste, their spirit of geometry, no comment. On their smartness, politeness, brilliant studies, no comment. On their kids' kids, no comment. On their screens and keyboards, their miraculous pictures, no comment. Normal road, penal code, no comment. On handsome chiefs, round-tables, unwritten rules, no comment. On their country before the law, the pursuit of happiness, natural borders, no comment. On margin, edge, and want, no comment. On our hammerhead gods, our obscure narratives, no comment.

ʼ

Sail ho. Quite
undeserved, black or white,
it moves past.
A sea of storm and war
below our battlements.
Like a wherefore of night,
a dungeon hole.

translated by Rosmarie Waldrop

AMONG THE PIGS

1.

The hog's surprised to find the door is open. He's just consumed his latest marriage to the sow that's tethered to the post, and now, in the 4 o'clock light, munches his turds, snorting. This is the song of a pig, three years old, without past, without passport, who turns his fat ass to the sun and means no harm. On the contrary: 1. his playful intelligence quickens freedom; 2. deep shit, his answer to the rage of the living.

2.

When the hog finds the door open, he charges into the heart of the orchard. Does he even notice the primroses, foxgloves, and cherries in season? Does he beware the wire hanging down to the ground though it isn't live? How sprightly this hog, this conqueror! How he rolls in the mud by the brook! This is information from a world now lost, from evenings around the fire with talk of pigs droning on and on. How can I tell you how outrageously pigs suffer nowadays? My distant childhood, which was not what you think, is stocked with a universal pig.

3.

This pig runs off squealing, chased by mamm-gozh in black, who wields a stick from the woodpile. I should just stay with this image. If my heart's in my mouth it's because I realized only later how different the new ways would be. Later, long after the noisy romp of hog and grandma in her work clothes — both proclaiming loudly the right to insurrection.

4.

As soon as my lips touch the bristle, I suspect the pig feels twice as important: 1. he's a prisoner of language. 2. stuck in garbage, life's a disaster. To start with, he doesn't even get to see either electric or barbed wire. Next, his sex life is not eliminated, but certainly curtailed. How hide the big knife behind our back? Social life mired in excrement. I worry when I see these pigs now. Feel like screaming: not this. Feel like thinking great crimes.

5.

I wonder if the knife doesn't simply have a stake in jerking in its sheath. Knowing what will happen. Happy ignorance in the 4 o'clock afternoon sun. At it with four hands. The guts intended for the parish. Under these conditions it's madness to get attached to the beast.

6.

Pig, are you there? I put on my pants, I put on my vest. To get into the new century I put on socks for good measure. The farmyard well-kept and swept, with tractor, field-roller, car. A sky of blood, thick as a scab. I put on my white apron. I take the pig in my arms, the pig wrapped in white towels. You must have loved to understand inner peace.

translated by Rosmarie Waldrop

THE BERLIN WALL
or
BLACKBERRY PICKING IN WESTERN BRITTANY

1.

What's this   the bent apple tree
        the black path
the faces never licked by love
                    five more days
        and I won't have to sing without love
            to dance   to pace
the sullen garden that sticks to my shoes

sunday on the grass
        red-cheeked desire
dramas of gods in the green field
        eternally misinterpreted
            choked
one sleeping in the arms of the other

the crow sinks
                and reappears
        clouds behind the apples
        clouds
of poetical bric-a-brac
                after you my little ones
the greatest dangers gulped down

travelers   it's enough to make you shout   howl
standing on the threshold
                the let-them-eat-cake maker
the baker and the little bakerboy[1]
                greet each other
with floured hands

someone is dead   his wife is dead
        in my dreams they talk
with an accidental voice
        huge upheavals in the tongue
                striking idiolects

not much joy in politics
if you compare us to the heroes of our youth
        full of dread
                we thought they'd give us
our weapons and our silence

2.

Come into the potato fields
          she says
and my ankles twist on the clods   on the stems
no rose on the rose tree
          romance writers always
let's watch the beautiful cars pass
          the hands of our dead
     in suits or Sunday dresses
          the sharp nose
     of her you still call
by pet names you'll never say again

     I drink from the tap
I piss on the wall of the stable
a pale yellow jet which erodes
          you've taken me by the hand
you speak to me of Belzec and Maïdanek

chance doesn't exclude lucidity
               we are
just steps from nightfall at the river
          fishing lines trailing
that summer night imagined
          for no other end
               than improvising
on the theme of Sweeney and Salaün

historicity   dynamic elements   philosophies
        of exploitation
                a little bit further
into the social sciences
I reach my right hand toward the moon
        toward the solid light of the stars
everything on the edge
            of coming apart

come   she says
        into formica kitchens
            my song of inexactness
by long practice on the tablecloth
it's a little autobiographical
               of course
the nice warm pans and the coffeepot

you remember the beginnings of the written world
you size up the processes
        great divide
        horizontal conceptions of time
I lived a double life
        tongue doubled   self doubled
             suicide
        today hair grows
            on the backs of my hands
            in my nostrils
I see my fingers ageing as I write

picking blackberries in the month of August
milk jugs   buckets   plastic bins
                              you move along
singing songs from the radio
                   a girl pees
           behind a telephone pole
this is the downfall of a world without morals
                                     force replayed
                   a vision of pure water
this is the always murky road
                              to arrive at each word
I didn't need blackberry picking
            but I like it
                      and it doesn't bother anyone

3.

The great glut of potato bugs
        is how I think of this garden
                    overturned wheelbarrow
            lessiveuse[2]
beneath a structure of flying colors
        the laundry line coated in gold
oh sweet therapist
        from hutch to coop
since the path with a view of the sea
                I have a neurosis at heart
in times of mass production

desire devours censure
        austerity of the watch
disparate dreams which is their specialty
                sorrow commands
it's a bad bargain
it's a tale that begins
                among flies
        pylons and posts
receive the calls
                the town embodies
        the irony
now that the prophecies are fulfilled
        damned damned country
tricks the blue sky
tricks death in dreams
                come closer   she says
        the little urchin swapped
for the excellence of ire and fury

midway through the cabbages
                our shadow grows
a shadow made of cabbages
       from *ker* to here
           subjecting the path
to our channeled words
         minimum of space
         angry gestures
against an infamous dualism
        walking
     in spirit through the cabbage
          doesn't get my feet less wet
I write to soak my feet among the cabbage

ladybugs of memory
          the bounding of *lessiveuses*
    the swallows like affect
             here and there   I am
affected by what's inert in the language
       I speak with the backdrop
         of capitalist   deployment
now irresistible
          in a country by the sea
taking to the pedals against the wind
        you spit out your soul
     it hits you right on the mouth

4.
The stones
at ground level don't stay in place
my mother
used to make piles of them like we make
from potatoes
then come the apples
arranged in piles
for filling baskets
a lack of love   sticks to me
I stick out my tongue

the task of picking blackberries
is a task of simple pleasure
we gather the blackberries like we make love
old   young
eager   reluctant
along the rows
red fingers   purple palms
my interest
in blackberry picking in Western Brittany
in the twenty-first century
its connections to
the production of symbols
the sharp gesture
that beats back thorns

lessiveuse
> no one knows anymore
> what a *lessiveuse* is
underneath there was a pile of embers
> there was a tripod
> a wheelbarrow pushed through the woods
> > a fire under the gray sky I see as blue
mute laundress
> the scandal of vivid colors
> in the icy basin water
I take a shortcut through the woods
it's me   I   do you want me to say it again   I
> take a shortcut through the woods
> by some kind of calculation
toward the shining blue
> > where I lost my place

5.

Images on motorcycles of our historical
reality
teeth gritted against the wind
grey sea lights up a furrow of blood
simple gesture of riding
as close as possible to the ditches
towards the life in the fields
clods   tubers   stems
scattered or in piles

in the fields after days of rumors
a strike from conformity
it's enough to make you laugh
they destroyed us
with a conformity of strikes
punctures   falls   predicaments
you push back   you tear
with hoes   with pickaxes
ways to break
with what's identical

garages where the oil rots in puddles
mixes brightly with rivets
with sprockets
revelry in the bright green talus
tiny refusal
emotion in the tongue's debris
me as if
I had forever left the prey
for the predator

country where the drooling light
                    pushes crime
hunks of scrap metal I nudge with the tip of my foot
back into the oil from changes
                         bits of language
                between the puddles
        so early this morning   it's vast

blackberries passed through the mill
                    by an even turn of the crank
            color of the sun going down
with boats   pines   white houses
                    I stopped by to see you
        on the inside of the apple
this street for example
                barred at one end
        other flows
other limits to history
    a strike from universalism
                    great gods
the horrible bow to classicism

6.

Your horses on the slatted bridge
toward the frontier
against the forest

the song fires without a kick
you have no idea
made me suffer

garden of poppies and peonies
of irritant childhood memories

crooning is crap

7.

The blackberry harvest is
August's undoing
    in little colored gestures
        of course   I'm the one
kneeling before the brambles
    arms brushing the nettles
        the thistles
and I sit back with my hands full of sugar
    to listen to the thrush
I stand for the woman with her little dog
    retired grower
    to whom life has given no gifts
I could tell her she is beautiful
    I don't say anything
    we talk   hot weather
    Marianna 'r Vod
the old path hidden by brambles
    rushed
she goes on her way toward Penn ar Menez

    the blackberries in the salad bowl
    the blackberries in the plastic box
    warming

    miserly earth
made to swipe its claws
    to paint our mouths
    to blacken our teeth

I remember you no longer wanted
    your body
        stitched up   pierced breast
    I slept against

8.

A hundred meters from the wall
the birdsmith is the bird of fate
symbolic fabric   atrophied religion
            the street is full of it
        everything feeds off the ordinary
from the street where everyone is on the way to work
                roses and blackcurrants in november
seeds from the catalog

        I'm furious   to trade for that
you should remember the harsh seasons
                summer   spring
everything that touches the history of the world
        that watches you without being able to speak

        always the same story
                posthumous blossoming
        where a bird with no memory
        pleases gods delighted with grace

it plays itself out like theater

my love
        is the love of the owl
come to throw itself on the electric wires

9.
Come   she says
let's twist our ankles
        in the potato fields

        the bodies of the tribe
                walked off in smoke
        skies thrown to the wind
                fog rolling
circulation of blood

the body of the one I loved most
        no historical reality without her
        and what is yet more beautiful
                the entanglements
        the innocence
        the super superstructures

when you're a child your hand
        moves aside the faces
        that block the view   look
how these things happen
        borderlines
        arthritis
                badly written poems

someone told me you were gone
        frankly I don't understand
        anything about words
            that hollow
I forbid myself all other women
        goes without saying
            but where had you gone
      unseen   unread
          not even poetical

the potato fields
           and closer and closer
      the lack of cars
         identity up to here
bang bang   these memories
              are rabbits
      you pull out of a hat
        and then hooray

10.
The simple act of saying names
                like at the theater
        when you make
                words say things
    holding to your lips
                    a little photo

translated by Laura Marris

1."Le boulanger, la boulangère et le petit mitron" is what the French revo-
lutionaries called Louis XVI, Marie Antoinette, and their son, after Louis
XVI promised the crowd bread at Versailles.

2. A *lessiveuse* is a precursor to the washing machine. It was operated
with a hand crank, and a fire or hot coals heated the water.

ABALAMOUR:

Because or Down with Love

Breton *abalamour* = because
French *à bas l'amour* = down with love

I'm not looking to write phrases that glide, but phrases that scrape the paper, shrinking from marvels, sentences so spontaneous that no one knows how they end

when I'm running beneath American oaks and hickories, hurricane season, cicadas thickening the ceiling of branches, confessions at hand, but how to know if the hand speaks truth,

this one here, my hand, writes that I run beneath the oaks and hickories of America, but it knows there's a choice between running and writing, and besides what's this story of American hickories,

they frame the stage, of course, the one where way becomes highway, the one from Atlanta to Providence, and if the impulse strikes I'll get the car this instant, tonight I could sleep at Keith and Rosmarie's,

the mattress on the floor, the books filling the house, books even in the john, I say "john" to show my age — words are signatures, even if the poem doesn't always join

the two ends, you see trees while running, you don't always know their names, even after consulting the guide you get nowhere, except that the names are lovelier than the trees, like the American walnut or hickory whose relation to the hiccup remains unknown, and the squirrels run up and down its length, their claws on the bark make the sound

of little sewing machines, I hate the noises they make in their throats, when I imitate them they stop scrabbling, not fooled, but intrigued, and I want to chase them down, blustering after their butts,

it's pretty small, the butt of an American squirrel, you can run after it forever, even Poussette never caught one, Poussette, my Siamese cat, born in North Carolina, died

in Kimerc'h, I decorated her tomb with pebbles I gathered on the beach at Pentrez, I painted them all different colors and that summer the rosebush I planted flowered twice in front of the colored stones,

it's easy to write when you're not trying to become, the sounds aren't real sounds, the dead stay dead and they belong to you, they haven't finished their violence, when you're not paying attention

they suck your blood, doubtless afraid you'll forget them, afraid of the time that passes and the living who, without bias, without meaning to, create disorder everywhere in the name of order, you say life's a bitch, but there are tricks in language, why is life a bitch, why one hell of a life, why not question everything at once, scowling all around you, I hear already the murmur of a penny dreadful

it would begin under the leaves of a hickory one summer evening while the growls of hurricane Ophelia recede with the water, in the wreckage of Katrina I remember Isabel and Gloria,

the exile leads a double life, the word fear no longer makes me afraid, it's the word with dark glasses that used to marshal me, now dead, the word fear doesn't blackmail me anymore, no more explaining things to myself,

no poem besides the concrete, no poem, no story, the visit to the purple iris, the white wine sipped on the terrace, the mist on the outside of the glass stops at the level of the wine, you lift the glass by the base to save the dew, no more visits to the purple iris,

exile is the pre-condition, banality of the excess of tongues and the absence of language, an exile from squirrels flattened in the road, forests of towering telephone poles, I used to run, hurry,

now I advance at a snail's pace, at night the world becomes flat as a plate, and I'm not afraid to slip from it, odd conversations in the bedroom with the white walls,

I'll out my selves while I'm at it, the trains rattle past, the planes take off, piers and parking lots in a world that doesn't exist, under blue sky the tan skins circle the world — above all

don't stay put, above all don't stray too far, I run in the woods of North Carolina, between the birds you hear the ringing of phones, with a hop I avoid a long green snake,

write badly, that's what it takes, because you're convinced that all literature is baloney, but then all the prose and all the poetry, I'm running through woods where beauties run in many languages,

and since there are no fauns or nymphs under the miles of greenery, I lend the snake a certain delicacy of manners, fine movements that draw contours in the dust, what the snake writes

speaks in harmony with wooden houses lit from within by televisions and computer screens, it's the snake's lot to pass under car tires so cushioned with shocks they don't register the slightest tremor,

not only snakes, but toads, frogs, squirrels, opossums, raccoons, and wasps, gnats, dragonflies, moths, go ahead — weep, the South illuminated by its battlefields, the world over, the ambivalent losers have a lot to hide, their re-painted icons, scattered words don't make a language, you take yourself so seriously you don't learn how to live,

I think of yours truly, running in North Carolina woods, not really living, but not dead because running, exile, age and forgetting — stop, you'll make us cry, your muzzle in the mirror,

sharp pain in my side, there are moments when writing spins off only to fall clumsily into rhetoric, I still fall prey to the siren songs of the worst, I chop my prose into little bites,

it's the sty's lot to portray the spirit of the age, a thousand snouts fighting to gulp the right soup, a thousand butts shitting, the voices of pigs at feeding time sing louder than poetry,

we used to feed this to the pigs: a mixture of skim milk, boiled new potatoes and bran, you stirred it, up to your elbows in a cauldron, and you could eat it,

and now, if I wanted to speak of rabbits, I would start with the mother rabbits who eat their young, and us, we had to feed them, blade in hand, cutting dandelions for the box or (the) bag, it's vulgar to speak of pigs and rabbits, I don't know anything more beautiful than the vulgar, the urine smell of the hutch, the males who thump their butts against the ground, a whole life in a cage of rabbits,

it's vulgar to speak of dogs, but some philosophers lived like dogs and think like dogs, the older I get, the more I shuffle and dance in place and move my arms

tossing everything on the floor, isn't it a shame this literary aping, I'm happy in the car, the Blue Ridge three hours away, sixty miles an hour to keep big words at a distance,

ready to cry at a Cherokee sunset, the bad parts of the American sky, sad like generations of ancestors, confirmed, mustachioed, in their Sunday clothes,

ah, how I love the September 19th sun brightening the head of a blue jay whose black eyes tell a story, the sound of the car rolling on the asphalt, my hands on the wheel,

the memory of memories, there, we used to cut purple asters, there, we horsed around in the gullies, I glide down the road through the mountains in the midst of birds whose names I don't always know—

their cries through the lowered window create an emptiness, damned pursuit of happiness, at night you hear the bear beget the bear, the fox beget the fox, all the social fauna drink from the brooks,

through the open window the moon's mistake rattled by branches, many years ago, in a Blue Ridge motel — how did I get here while I was running in the fields,

while at the last second I sidestep the long green snake, very thin, who leaves his snake imprint in the dust, the order of words isn't reality, a page of writing demands continuity,

how can you write: I run, when you don't run it's easy to write: I run, you can write a poem in your head when you're running, but as soon as it's laid out on paper, funny expression,

only wind will remain, all poems fall from my hands, I expect the downtime to strike me, one late summer morning, post-hurricane, at the doctor's I finally understood that time doesn't die,

here, in the South, you cry each Sunday for judgment day, and what will you do when death in his tall hat comes to find you, obedient, you'll get into the carriage, the wik-ha-wak softened by a bed of sand, it will disappear into nothing, the afterlife is not life, there's no salvation in words, they never say anything but the impotence of saying,

there's the language of polished granite, adorned with a ceramic cherub who beats his wings, the urn of cold ashes lowered into the earth, and over the wall the bay drowned in light, the ships rising up against the wind,

in my head I have a field of buttercups, in spring the teacher led the class there singing, no photos exist of these moments, there's truth in photos, sometimes too much, so you hide them in the dresser,

there's no other afterlife except in photos, at the end of two generations what remains, whose wedding was that, the woman smirking with cold-water eyes, what was her name,

leaving traces, not leaving traces, the babies born with new forms, they are not yet enslaved to love, their eyes calm, their fists pushing away scratchy chins,

at the end of never-ending meals where everyone talks loudly they get the smacks they'll remember all their lives, the smell of dogs under the table, the hens in the hall, the sunken path changed to a flood, the sky of closed eyes, the formless searching for a form—new forms don't appear on the threshing floor despite the sound of the engine and the friction of the belts,

that evening, hearing my mother cry, I searched for the origin of her tears, I never saw my father cry, shout, yes, red-faced, mad at himself, my father never

knew irony, parody, derision, it was enough for him to believe the world would always be the world and the world was, what did he dream of, my father never knew the unconscious,

that goes without saying, no more than us my father never had any ambition but to obey, my mother was something else, in her senile madness she spoke to the dead, she spoke to God, she would have broken God

with a crowbar, she would have ordered him to prove his non-existence, my mother could have been God-made-woman, it's strange to think we've forever abandoned her large calloused hand,

I cannot stop talking to the dead, for a time after they die they smell like honey, I could not cry, I had to pull myself together, blow by blow, my life jumps from character to character, and I still root

for each of them, and there is no good reason for all of this, you have nothing to fear but the death of the tongue, how to represent its death, language carries within her an order that you can't command,

I no longer want a language of ties, I don't want a tongue that tears, such October heat, every second a memory begins, the gilded houses, the absence of wind, children's games

under the American oaks and hickories, with ears pressed to trunks they hear the trees talk amongst themselves, the kids know all about childhood memories, they forge them everyday

with appalling gaps, moving by the grace of blue sky, the boys leaping with loud cries on the trampoline sing chaos theory, I don't cast the stone

at the snake's child, I don't step on him, I push him away carefully with the help of a branch, let him slither toward the stream through the thick dead leaves, the man who ages

is like his father, he won't cry as he dies, relieved to rid himself of life, there is always an end to our episode, what do the adventures matter, it's the death rattle that searches the lower regions, the insides returning to the surface with the sound of tearing membrane, the father lovingly attended in the hospital room, in silence until the hour the sun brightens the hawthorns,

the dawn rises without a crow, the beauty of the world glides over the weeds, you tell yourself this day will be like all the others, with a morning and evening, you'll lie down in the afternoon, and in your sleep

there won't be a ghost, in the minority language there is no concept of minority, in the language of the majority everybody wants to be loved, all the love songs talk about terror,

the huge noise of insects outside, the huge, the marvelous North Carolina insects call out to each other in the night, racket of last judgment, forehead on the pane I try to see over the confusion of sounds —

the telephone rings, and it's Dublin, London, Paris calling, it took time to learn to live alone, when you say: that's life, you don't know what you're saying, is it *kiez ar bed, one hell of a life,*

you probably mean the stroke of luck, the accident, since all life is loss, how unfamiliar are the features of the women I loved, they hide their faces in their hands the traces you keep are the marks of slithering in the dust, a long green snake crossed the path, with a leap I avoided him, his sound of dead leaves in the woods,

the tail end of life, what can I make of it, not fear of death, not a storm, not the work of forgetting, not lofty wisdom, not florid words, not erudition, no, not for the world.

Durham, September 5 - October 5, 2005

translated by Laura Marris

BIONOTES

Paol Keineg was born in Brittany in 1944. His first book, *Le poème du pays qui a faim* [Poem of the famished land] of 1967, became a manifesto of Breton militancy against colonization by the French State and put him in the forefront of the new Breton literature. While remaining emotionally rooted in Brittany and intensely interested in Celtic mythology, he lived in the US for about thirty years, teaching at Brown and Duke, before returning to his native village in 2009. He is both playwright and poet and has translated Breton and American poets into French. His most recent books of poetry are a collected poems, *Les trucs sont démolis* (2008), *Abalamour* (2012), and *Mauvaises Langues* (2014). Burning Deck has published a translation of *Boudica*.

Laura Marris' work has appeared in *The Cortland Review, Asymptote, The Common, Boston Review Online,* and elsewhere. Her recent translations include Louis Guilloux's novel *Blood Dark* (forthcoming from the New York Review Books) and Christophe Boltanski's *The Safe House* (University of Chicago Press). She lives in Providence.

Rosmarie Waldrop has translated, from the German, Elke Erb, Friederike Mayröcker, Oskar Pastior, Gerhard Rühm, Ulf Stolterfoht, and, from the French, Edmond Jabès, Emmanuel Hocquard, and Jacques Roubaud. Her most recent book of poetry is *Gap Gardening: Selected Poems* (New Directions, 2016).